Ocean Animals

WALRUSES

By Benjamin Proudfit

Please visit our website, www.garethstevens.com. For a free color catalog of all our high-quality books, call toll free 1-800-542-2595 or fax 1-877-542-2596.

Library of Congress Cataloging-in-Publication Data

Names: Proudfit, Benjamin, author.
Title: Walruses / Benjamin Proudfit.
Description: New York : Gareth Stevens Publishing, [2020] | Series: Ocean animals
Identifiers: LCCN 2019010487| ISBN 9781538244739 (paperback) | ISBN 9781538244753 (library bound) | ISBN 9781538244746 (6 pack)
Subjects: LCSH: Walrus–Juvenile literature.
Classification: LCC QL737.P62 P76 2020 | DDC 599.79/9–dc23
LC record available at https://lccn.loc.gov/2019010487

First Edition

Published in 2020 by
Gareth Stevens Publishing
111 East 14th Street, Suite 349
New York, NY 10003

Designer: Katelyn E. Reynolds
Editor: Kristen Rajczak Nelson

Photo credits: Cover, pp. 1, 7, 24 (flippers) Vladimir Melnik/Shutterstock.com; pp. 5, 21, 24 (calf) tryton2011/Shutterstock.com; p. 9 Pole 2 Pole Images/Shutterstock.com; p. 11 JIANG HONGYAN/Shutterstock.com; p. 13 Vaclav Sebek/Shutterstock.com; pp. 15, 24 (tusk) Mikhail Cheremkin/Shutterstock.com; p. 17 Pavelvosolok/Shutterstock.com; p. 19 Aleksei Verhovski/Shutterstock.com; p. 23 Nyura/Shutterstock.com.

Printed in the United States of America

CPSIA compliance information: Batch #CW20GS: For further information contact Gareth Stevens, New York, New York at 1-800-542-2595.

Contents

Where Are Walruses? 4

What They Look Like . . . 12

Living Together 16

See One! 22

Words to Know 24

Index 24

Walruses live
in the ocean!

They have flippers
for swimming.
They can walk
on land, too!

They live in the cold.

They eat clams.

They are brown
and pink.

They have long teeth.
These are tusks.

They live in big groups.
These are herds.

They make lots of noise!

A baby is called a calf.

You may see one
at the zoo!

Words to Know

calf flipper tusk

Index

baby 20
body 6, 12, 14
food 10
herds 16